HOW DID WE FIND OUT ABOUT
ATOMS?

HOW DID WE FIND OUT . . . SERIES
Each of the books in this series on the history of science
emphasizes the process of discovery.

How Did We Find Out . . . ?
Books by Isaac Asimov

HOW DID WE FIND OUT

ABOUT ATOMS?

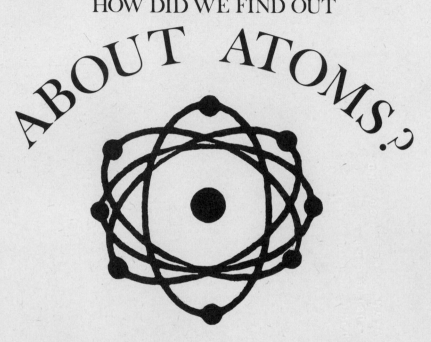

Isaac Asimov
Illustrated by David Wool

WALKER AND COMPANY
New York

To the beautiful Leslie Bennetts, from her
taller-than-her cousin-by-marriage

First published in the United States of America
in 1976 by the Walker Publishing Company, Inc.

Published simultaneously in Canada by Fitzhenry &
Whiteside, Limited, Toronto.

TRADE ISBN: 0-8027-6247-6

REINF. ISBN: 0-8027-6248-4

Library of Congress Catalog Card Number: 75-3910

Printed in the United States of America.

10 9 8 7 6 5 4 3 2 1

Contents

1 The Notion of Atoms

HAVE YOU EVER looked at a sandy beach from a distance? It seems like a solid piece of material, doesn't it?

If you come close to it, though, you can see that it is made up of small, hard pieces of sand. You can pick up some of the beach sand and let it trickle through your fingers. You can let all of it go except for one small grain you might keep in your palm.

Is that small grain the smallest piece of sand there can be? Suppose you put that small grain on a very hard rock and hit it with a hammer. Wouldn't you smash it into smaller pieces? Couldn't you smash one of those smaller pieces into still smaller pieces? Could you keep on doing that forever?

Or suppose you took a sheet of paper and tore it in half. Then suppose you tore the half-sheet in half again, and that new smaller piece in half, and so on? Could you keep on doing *that* forever?

Two thousand five hundred years ago, about 450 B.C., a Greek scholar, or "philosopher," thought

7

about these questions. His name was Leucippus (lyoo-SIP-us). It didn't make sense to him to suppose that anything could be broken into smaller, and smaller, and smaller pieces forever. Somewhere there had to come an end. At some point you had to reach a piece so small that it couldn't be broken up into anything smaller.

Leucippus had a pupil, Democritus (dee-MOK-rih-tus), who also thought this way. By the time Democritus died in 380 B.C., he had written some seventy-two books about his theories of the universe. Among the theories was the idea that everything in the world was made up of very tiny pieces that were too small to be broken up further.

Democritus's name for these small pieces was "atomos," which is a Greek word meaning "unbreakable." That word becomes "atom" in English.

Democritus thought the whole world was made up of different kinds of atoms and that in between the atoms there was nothing at all. The separate atoms were too small to be seen, but when many of them were joined in different combinations, they made up all the different things we see about us. He thought atoms couldn't be made or destroyed, although they could change their arrangements. In that way, one substance would be changed into another.

Democritus couldn't say why he believed all this. It just seemed to make sense to him. But to most other Greek philosophers it did *not* seem to make sense. Indeed, the most famous Greek philosophers did not think atoms existed and Democritus's views, which we might call "atomism," therefore became unpopular.

DEMOCRITUS
(460-380 B.C.)

9

In ancient times, all books were handwritten. In order to have more than one copy of a particular book, the whole book had to be copied by hand. It was very hard work, and only very popular books were copied a large number of times.

Since Democritus's books were not popular, few copies were made. As time went on, copy after copy was lost. Today, not one single copy of any of his books exists. They are all completely gone. The only reason we know about his theories is that other ancient books, which have survived, mention Democritus and refer to his theory of the atoms.

Before Democritus's books were entirely lost, however, another Greek philosopher, Epicurus (ep-ih-KYOO-rus), read them and became an atomist himself. In 306 B.C., he established a school in Athens, Greece, which was then an important teaching center. Epicurus was a popular teacher and he was the first to let women come into his school as students. He taught that all things were made up of atoms, and he is supposed to have written no less than three hundred books on various subjects (although ancient books were usually quite short).

In the long run, though, Epicurus's views also lost popularity and his books were copied fewer and fewer times. In the end, they were all lost, just like those of Democritus.

But the notion of atoms didn't disappear. Two centuries after Epicurus, while his books still existed, a Roman scholar, Lucretius (lyoo-KREE-shus), became an atomist. He, too, thought that the world was made up of atoms. About 56 B.C., he wrote a long poem in Latin whose title in English is *On the Na-*

ture of Things. In that poem, he explained the views of Democritus and Epicurus in considerable detail and with great skill.

Just the same, the notion of atoms never seemed to be popular. Lucretius's poem wasn't copied often, either. As the civilization of Greece and Rome broke down, copy after copy disappeared, until finally there wasn't a single one left. By the time of the Middle Ages in Europe, all the writings of Democritus, Epicurus, and Lucretius were gone and people had forgotten about atoms.

Then, in 1417, someone came across an old manuscript in an attic, which turned out to be a somewhat damaged copy of Lucretius's poem. No other copy from ancient times was ever found. By that time, though, people in Europe had become very interested in all ancient writings, so, when this manuscript was discovered, it was promptly copied a number of times.

In 1454, a German named Johann Gutenberg (GOO-ten-burg) invented printing. Instead of being copied by hand, all the words of a book were set up in type. Then copy after copy could be printed by inking the type and pressing sheets of paper against it. In this way, many copies of every book could be quickly made. There was much less danger of books disappearing after that.

One of the first books to be put into printed form was Lucretius's poem. Many Europeans read the poem and some were impressed by the notion of atoms. One of them was a French scholar named Pierre Gassendi (ga-sahn-DEE), who wrote several influential books in the first half of the 1600s. He

THE GUTENBERG PRESS

knew many of the other scholars in Europe at the time and informed them of his views on atoms.

In this way, the original notions of Leucippus survived for two thousand years. Atomism just barely made it into modern times, thanks to the lucky finding of that one copy of Lucretius's poem. Of course, modern scientists probably would have thought of atoms themselves, but it helped to have the idea ready-made from ancient times.

During the entire stretch of two thousand years, however, there was one point that kept atoms from being taken seriously by most scholars. Atoms were only a *notion*. They were just something that seemed logical to some people.

There was no *evidence*. Nobody could say, "Here is something that behaves in a particular manner. The only way of explaining the behavior is to suppose that atoms exist."

To find such evidence, people had to conduct experiments. They had to study the behavior of matter under certain conditions, in order to test whether that behavior could be explained by atoms, or not.

Gassendi was one of the first to suggest that the proper way of learning about the universe was to carry out experiments. Among the people who knew of Gassendi's views was an English chemist, Robert Boyle. He was the first scientist to conduct experiments that seemed to show atoms might exist.

Boyle was interested in air, for instance, and in how it behaved. Air wasn't a solid that was hard to the touch and kept its shape. It wasn't a liquid, like water, that flowed but could be seen. It was a mate-

ROBERT BOYLE
(1627-1691)

rial that spread out very thinly. Such a material is called a "gas."

In 1662, Boyle poured a little mercury (a liquid metal) into a seventeen-foot-long glass tube shaped like the letter J. The end of the short part of the tube was closed, while the long part was left open.

The mercury filled the bottom part of the J and the air was trapped in the short, closed part of the tube. Boyle then poured more mercury into the tube. The weight of the additional mercury forced some of it up into the short part. As the mercury was forced in, the trapped air was squeezed into a smaller space. It was "compressed." The more mercury Boyle added, the more the trapped air was compressed into a smaller and smaller space.

Boyle worked out how the space taken up by the air grew less with the increasing weight of mercury. This is called "Boyle's law."

But how can air be compressed? How can it be squeezed into a smaller space?

A sponge can be compressed into a smaller space. So can a piece of bread. This is because the sponge or the bread has little holes in it. When you squeeze the sponge or the bread, you squeeze the air out of those holes and bring the solid material of the sponge, or the bread, closer together. (If you squeeze a wet sponge, you push water out of the holes.)

If you can squeeze air together, as Boyle did, it must mean that the air has holes in it. In squeezing, you close those holes and bring the material of the air closer together.

It seemed to Boyle that there must be little pieces

BOYLE'S EXPERIMENT

of air—tiny atoms. Between the atoms there was space containing nothing at all. When air was compressed, the atoms were forced closer together. He felt this was true for all gases.

In fact, it might apply to liquids and solids, too. If you boil liquid water, it will turn into steam, which is a gas. If you cool the steam you get water again.

The steam takes up over a thousand times as much space as the water. The easiest way of explaining this is to suppose that in water all the atoms are so close they are touching, while in steam they are far apart.

Thus, with Boyle, in 1662, atoms for the first time became more than just a notion.

Steam or water vapor molecules

Liquid water molecules

THE ANCIENT GREEK
IDEA OF ELEMENTS

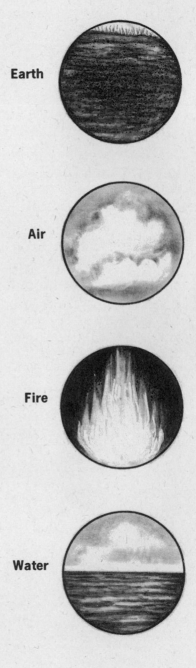

Earth

Air

Fire

Water

2 The Evidence of Atoms

COULD THERE BE different kinds of atoms?

Democritus had thought there might be. The ancient Greeks believed the world was made up of four kinds of basic matter, or "elements." These were earth, water, air, and fire. Democritus felt each one of them might have a different kind of atom.

The earth atoms might be rough and uneven, so that they stuck together easily and formed the solid earth. The water atoms might be smooth and round, so that they slipped past each other and water could flow. The air atoms might be very feathery, so that they floated. The fire atoms might be pointy and jagged, which was why fire hurt.

The Greeks, however, had chosen the four elements only because they seemed to make sense. They had no evidence that the world was really made up of them.

Boyle, in a book he wrote in 1661, said that elements must be discovered by experiment. Chemists must try to break down everything to the simplest possible substances. Once they had something that couldn't be broken down any further, *that* was an element.

After Boyle's book was published, chemists began to look for elements by experimenting with matter. By the end of the 1700s, they had discovered about thirty different elements.

Most of the common metals, such as copper, silver, gold, iron, tin, lead, and mercury, are elements. These metals were known to the ancients, but the chemists of the 1700s also found new metal elements, such as nickel, cobalt (KOH-bawlt), and uranium (yoo-RAY-nee-um).

The chemists also discovered that air is a mixture of two gases, oxygen (OK-sih-jen) and nitrogen (NI-troh-jen). Each is an element. Another gas that is an element is hydrogen (HI-droh-jen). There are also elements that are neither metals nor gases. Carbon, sulfur, and phosphorus (FOS-foh-rus) are examples of these.

Could it be that every element has a different kind of atom? Could there be silver atoms and nickel atoms and oxygen atoms and sulfur atoms?

Throughout the 1700s, few chemists thought about this. Although Boyle and some others were atomists, most chemists were not. They searched for new elements and studied the way in which these behaved. They didn't concern themselves with atoms, because they didn't see any use in trying to study tiny objects that couldn't be seen.

Still, the evidence for atoms piled up. Some was obtained by a French chemist, Antoine Laurent La-

ANTOINE LAURENT LAVOISIER
(1743-1794)

voisier (lah-vwah-ZYAY). He discovered, in 1782, that when one substance is changed into another, as when wood is burned in air and becomes ash and smoke, the total weight doesn't change. The final ash and smoke weigh as much as the original wood and air. This is called "the law of conservation of matter."

Lavoisier was not one of those chemists who concerned himself about atoms, but his discovery did fit the notion.

Suppose Democritus was right. Suppose atoms can't be made or destroyed, and all that can be done is to change their arrangement. Wood and air would contain atoms in one kind of arrangement. When the wood was burned, the atoms would change their arrangement to form ash and smoke. All the atoms would still be there, though, and their total weight wouldn't change.

If that is so, we can test the matter further. Instead of weighing everything, we might weigh each separate element and see what happens when we change things around.

A French chemist, Joseph Louis Proust (PROOST), tried this. He worked in Spain because a violent revolution began in France in 1789 and he thought it was safer to leave. (It was. Poor Lavoisier didn't leave and he had his head cut off in 1794.)

One thing Proust found was that he could combine three elements, copper, carbon, and oxygen, to form a "compound" called copper carbonate (KAHR-bohnate). (A compound is a substance made up of a combination of different elements.)

To do this, he took five ounces of copper, four ounces of oxygen, and one ounce of carbon. He ended up with ten ounces of copper carbonate, since the total weight couldn't change.

Proust found, however, that no matter what system he used to put these elements together, he always had to use the same proportions. It was always five of copper to four of oxygen to one of carbon. If he began with other proportions, one or two of the elements was always left over.

Proust went on to show that this was true of other compounds as well. They were always built out of elements in certain definite proportions and no other. By 1799, Proust was certain this was true of all compounds. His discovery is called "the law of definite proportions."

PROUST COMBINED THESE ELEMENTS TO MAKE COPPER CARBONATE.

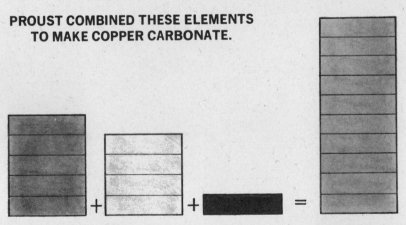

5 units copper + 4 units oxygen + 1 unit carbon = 10 units copper carbonate

Proust didn't concern himself about atoms, but you can see where they fit in here. Suppose all the elements were made up of atoms, and the atoms couldn't be broken into smaller pieces. When elements joined to form some compound, so many atoms of one element would combine with so many atoms of another.

This connection between atoms and the law of definite proportions occurred to an English chemist, John Dalton. He was interested in gases and was very familiar with the experiments of Boyle. He could see that the best way to explain how air and other gases behave is to suppose they are made up of atoms. He could also see that the law of definite proportions made sense if you suppose all the elements are made up of atoms.

Dalton studied the combination of elements on his own and he came across something new. Sometimes two elements combined in different proportions after all. For instance, three ounces of carbon combine with four ounces of oxygen to form a certain gas. On the other hand, three ounces of carbon combine with eight ounces of oxygen to form a different gas.

The proportions are different, but you'll notice that eight is just twice as large as four. Dalton wondered if, in the first case, one atom of carbon combined with one atom of oxygen, while in the second case one atom of carbon combined with two atoms of oxygen.

The names we have for the two gases nowadays suits this thought. Three ounces of carbon and four ounces of oxygen make "carbon monoxide" (mon-

JOHN DALTON
(1766-1844)

OK-side), while three ounces of carbon and eight ounces of oxygen make "carbon dioxide" (di-OK-side). The prefix "mon" means "one" and "di" means "two."

Dalton found other cases like this. One ounce of hydrogen can combine with three ounces of carbon to form a gas called methane (METH-ane). One ounce of hydrogen can combine with six ounces of carbon to form a gas called ethylene (ETH-ih-leen). Again, notice that six is twice as large as three.

Whenever Dalton found elements combining in different proportions, the higher proportions were always simple multiples of the lower ones—they were twice as large or three times as large. Dalton's discovery is called "the law of multiple proportions" and he announced it in 1803.

Dalton could see that the law of multiple proportions made sense if you considered that one atom or two atoms or three atoms of one element could combine with one atom of another element, but never two and a half atoms or anything like that. He thought this was the final bit of evidence needed to show that elements combined as atoms that could not be broken down into smaller pieces.

In 1808, Dalton published a book in which he described his views on atoms. Because of this book, it is Dalton who is usually given credit for working out the "atomic theory" and for having discovered atoms.

This may seem strange to you, since his views were the same as those of Leucippus and Democritus over two thousand years before. Why aren't those ancient Greek philosophers given the credit?

There is a difference, you see. Leucippus and Democritus were just expressing their opinions. They had no evidence, so no one had to believe them, and, in fact, hardly anyone did.

Dalton, however, went over all the chemical experiments that could be easily explained by supposing that atoms existed. He showed how they could be used to explain Boyle's law, the law of conservation of matter, the law of definite proportions, and the law of multiple proportions.

When the notion of atoms can explain so many different findings, and these findings can't be explained in any other way, then it is hard to deny the notion. Now people began to believe that atoms did indeed exist. After Dalton published his book, more and more chemists came to accept the notion of atoms and soon almost all chemists did. That is why it is Dalton who gets the credit for the atomic theory.

3

The
Weight
of Atoms

DALTON WONDERED what made the atoms of different elements different from each other.

The experiments that men like Lavoisier, Proust, and Dalton himself had carried out involved the weight of different substances. Perhaps it was possible to work out the weights of the different atoms. Perhaps that was what made atoms different from each other.

No one could weigh a single atom, of course. It was too tiny to see and certainly too tiny to work with. Maybe, though, the weights of different atoms could be compared with each other.

For instance, one ounce of hydrogen combines with eight ounces of oxygen to form water. Suppose you consider the simplest atom arrangement for water—one hydrogen atom combined with one oxygen atom. In that case, it must mean that each oxygen atom is eight times as heavy as each hydrogen atom. If you let 1 represent the weight of the hydrogen atom, you would have to let 8 represent the weight of the oxygen atom.

Dalton went on to compare the weights of other combinations of elements and to work out how heavy each atom was in comparison to hydrogen. (Hydrogen turned out to be made up of the lightest of all the atoms.)

However, Dalton had made a mistake. It turned out that water was not made up of one hydrogen atom for every oxygen atom. This was found out in the following way.

In 1800, an Italian scientist, Alessandro Volta (VOLE-tuh), had put together the first electric battery. It produced an electric current that could be made to pass through certain substances. Before the year was over, an English chemist, William Nicholson, heard of the discovery. He built a battery of his own and passed an electric current through water.

Nicholson found that when an electric current passed through water, the water was broken down into hydrogen and oxygen. He collected the two gases separately and found that the volume of hydrogen (the room it took up) was twice as great as the volume of oxygen.

In 1809, a French chemist, Joseph Louis Gay-Lussac (gay-lyoo-SAK), found that gases always seemed to combine in volumes that could be written as small whole numbers. When hydrogen and oxygen combined to form water, the volume of hydrogen was just twice the volume of oxygen. When hydrogen and chlorine (KLAW-reen) combined to form hydrogen chloride (KLAW-ride), the volume of hydrogen was equal to the volume of chlorine. When nitrogen

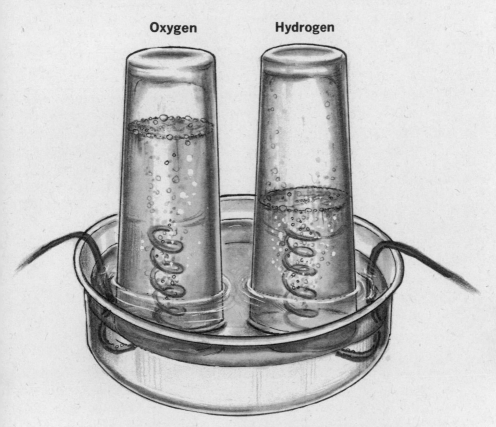

Oxygen   **Hydrogen**

An electric current passed through water breaks down the water into hydrogen and oxygen. The volume of hydrogen on the right is twice as much as the volume of oxygen on the left.

and hydrogen combined to form ammonia (uh-MOH-nee-uh), the volume of hydrogen was just three times that of nitrogen. This is called "the law of combining volumes."

In 1811, an Italian physicist, Amedeo Avogadro (ah-voh-GAH-droh), decided he could explain the law of combining volume, if the same volume of different gases was always made up of the same number of particles. These particles might be individual atoms, or they might be combinations of atoms called "molecules" (MOL-uh-kyoolz). This is called "Avogadro's hypothesis" (hi-POTH-ih-sis). The word "hypothesis" means a suggestion.

If this hypothesis was correct, since two volumes of hydrogen combine with one volume of oxygen, that would probably mean that *two* hydrogen atoms and one oxygen atom combine to form a molecule of water, instead of one each as Dalton had thought.

The amount of oxygen used in forming water is still eight times as heavy as the amount of hydrogen. This means that the oxygen atom in the water molecule must weigh eight times as much as the two hydrogen atoms put together. An oxygen atom must then weigh sixteen times as much as a single hydrogen atom. If we represent the weight of hydrogen as 1, the weight of oxygen must be 16.

Chemists came to accept the presence of two hydrogen atoms in the water molecule, but almost nobody paid attention to Avogadro's hypothesis. For about fifty years, chemists didn't quite understand what the law of multiple proportions meant.

By the 1810s so many chemists were talking about

AMEDEO AVOGADRO
(1776-1856)

elements and atoms, that they felt they really needed some shorthand way of describing them. It was so complicated always to say "a water molecule made up of two atoms of hydrogen and one atom of oxygen," whenever they wanted to talk about the particles composing water.

Dalton had used little circles to represent atoms. He drew the atoms of each different element as a different kind of circle. One element was just a blank circle, another was a black circle, still another was a circle with a dot in it, and so on. To show how different atoms combined to form compounds, he put different circles together. It was a kind of code that quickly got very difficult to use, as more elements and compounds needed to be represented.

A Swedish chemist, Jöns Jakob Berzelius (bur-ZEE-lee-us), had a better idea in 1813. He suggested that each element be represented by the initial letter of its Latin name. If two elements began with the same letter, a second letter from the name could be used. That would be the "chemical symbol," standing for the element and also standing for one atom of the element.

Thus, oxygen could be represented as O, nitrogen as N, carbon as C, hydrogen as H, chlorine as Cl, sulfur as S, phosphorus as P, and so on. When the Latin names were different from the English ones, the symbol wasn't as clear. Since the Latin word for gold is "aurum," for example, the chemical symbol for gold is "Au."

By using Berzelius's system, it became easy to show the molecules of various substances. For in-

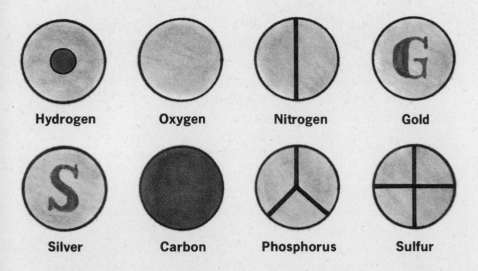

Hydrogen   Oxygen   Nitrogen   Gold

Silver   Carbon   Phosphorus   Sulfur

DALTON'S CODE

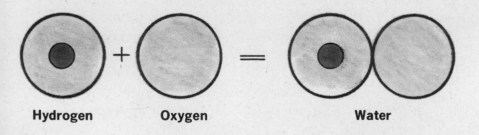

Hydrogen   +   Oxygen   =   Water

stance, H represents a single hydrogen atom, but it was found that hydrogen gas wasn't made up of single atoms. It was made up of molecules, each one of which was composed of two hydrogen atoms. The molecule could be written as H_2.

Other elements in gaseous form were also found to occur as two-atom molecules. You could write O_2, N_2, and Cl_2 for the oxygen molecule, the nitrogen molecule, and the chlorine molecule.

It was just as easy to write the symbols for molecules made up of more than one kind of atom. Since the water molecule is made up of two hydrogen atoms and one oxygen atom, it could be written as H_2O. Carbon dioxide, with molecules made up of one carbon atom and two oxygen atoms, is CO_2, while carbon monoxide is CO.

Berzelius spent many years measuring the exact weights of the different elements that combined to form particular compounds, just as Proust had done. Berzelius tested more compounds than Proust had, however, and was able to work more accurately.

Berzelius used his measurements to work out the weights of the atoms of the various elements. In 1828, he published a table of what came to be called "atomic weights." For the most part, Berzelius's table was accurate, but, unfortunately, he didn't pay any attention to Avogadro's hypothesis about equal volumes of gases having equal numbers of particles. For that reason, he was led astray in some cases and got two or three atomic weights completely wrong.

Others were misled as well and for a long time different chemists insisted on different atomic weights

JÖNS JAKOB BERZELIUS
(1779-1848)

for certain elements. Some were confused between the hydrogen atom (H) and the hydrogen molecule (H_2), and between other cases of this kind.

By the 1850s, there were so many arguments about the structure of different molecules and about how to write the formulas, that it began to look as though the whole notion of atoms would have to be discarded. Atomism couldn't be right if it gave rise to so much trouble.

A German chemist, Friedrich August Kekulé (KAY-koo-lay), thought the best thing to do was to get all the chemists in Europe together and have them argue it out. In 1860, therefore, the First International Chemical Congress was held in the town of Karlsruhe (KAHRLZ-roo-uh) in Germany. It was the first international meeting of scientists ever held. One hundred and forty chemists attended from Germany, France, Great Britain, Russia, Italy, and other nations.

One of those attending was an Italian chemist, Stanislao Cannizzaro (kahn-need-DZAH-roh). He knew all about Avogadro's hypothesis and he was convinced that, if chemists paid attention to it, they would all be much better off.

He prepared all his thoughts in a clearly written pamphlet. At the Congress, he made a strong speech about Avogadro, then handed out his pamphlet to all the chemists present. He also talked in private to some of the more important ones, explaining all the points carefully.

His efforts worked. The chemists understood, and the confusion of the past years began to go away.

At the time, a Belgian chemist, Jean Servais Stas,

FRIEDRICH AUGUST KEKULÉ
(1829-1896)

was working out a table of atomic weights with greater care than even Berzelius had done. He worked so carefully that he could show that the oxygen atom was not exactly sixteen times as heavy as the hydrogen atom. It was a little less heavy than that. If the hydrogen atom was 1, then the oxygen atom was 15.88.

Oxygen, however, combined with more of the various elements than hydrogen did, so that Stas worked with oxygen almost all the time. It was very convenient for him to have the atomic weight of oxygen an even number. It made the arithmetic easier. Stas let the atomic weight of oxygen be exactly 16, which meant the atomic weight of hydrogen would be 1.008, instead of 1. This system continued to be used for a hundred years.

Stas adopted Avogadro's hypothesis after Cannizzaro explained it at the conference. Stas prepared his atomic weights accordingly and by 1865 he was able to make public the first modern table of such figures. Since that time, there have been corrections to his figures, but only small ones.

4 The Arrangement of Atoms

ALTHOUGH THE PROBLEM of the atomic weights was now worked out, that wasn't the only difficulty in connection with atoms.

Most of the compounds studied in the early 1800s were made up of simple molecules with just a few atoms in each. It was enough to list the different kinds of atoms and tell how many there were of each. The water molecule was H_2O (two atoms of hydrogen and one atom of oxygen); the ammonia molecule was NH_3 (one atom of nitrogen and three atoms of hydrogen); the hydrogen chloride molecule was HCl (one atom of hydrogen and one atom of chlorine); the molecule of sulfuric acid was H_2SO_4 (two atoms of hydrogen, one atom of sulfur, and four atoms of oxygen).

In some cases, however, just numbering the atoms wasn't enough. In 1824, two German chemists, Justus von Liebig (LEE-big) and Friedrich Wöhler (VOI-ler), were working on two different compounds. Each worked out the formula for his compound, and found so many atoms of this element and so many of that.

When they announced their results, it turned out that both compounds had the same formula. The molecule of each contained the same elements in the same proportions—yet they were different compounds behaving in different ways.

Berzelius, who was the leading chemist of his time, was astonished. He repeated the work of the two chemists and found that both were correct. There *were* two different compounds made up of the same elements in the same proportions. Berzelius called them "isomers" (EYE-soh-murz), from Greek words meaning "equal proportions."

Other cases of isomers were found, almost always in molecules containing the carbon atom. This was particularly important because the molecules present in living organisms usually contain carbon atoms. In fact, Berzelius called these carbon-containing molecules from plants and animals "organic compounds" for that reason.

It became harder and harder to work out the formulas for organic compounds. Whereas most of the molecules without carbon atoms ("inorganic compounds") were small, so that their structures were easily worked out, organic compounds were made up of large molecules containing many atoms. Chemists began to grow very confused as to just how many of each type of atom were present in the large organic molecules. Even when they did come out with some figures, they found that the same combinations, C_2H_6O, for instance, might represent several different isomers.

THE ELEMENTS, THEIR SYMBOLS, ATOMIC NUMBERS, AND ATOMIC WEIGHTS

Name of element	Sym-bol	Atomic number	Atomic weight	Name of element	Sym-bol	Atomic number	Atomic weight
Actinium	Ac	89	[227]	Mercury	Hg	80	200.59
Aluminum	Al	13	26.9815	Molybdenum	Mo	42	95.94
Americium	Am	95	[243]	Neodymium	Nd	60	144.24
Antimony	Sb	51	121.75	Neon	Ne	10	20.183
Argon	Ar	18	39.948	Neptunium	Np	93	[237]
Arsenic	As	33	74.9216	Nickel	Ni	28	58.71
Astatine	At	85	[210]	Niobium	Nb	41	92.906
Barium	Ba	56	137.34	Nitrogen	N	7	14.0067
Berkelium	Bk	97	[249*]	(Nobelium)	(No)	102	
Beryllium	Be	4	9.0122	Osmium	Os	76	190.2
Bismuth	Bi	83	208.980	Oxygen	O	8	15.9994
Boron	B	5	10.811	Palladium	Pd	46	106.4
Bromine	Br	35	79.909	Phosphorus	P	15	30.9738
Cadmium	Cd	48	112.40	Platinum	Pt	78	195.09
Calcium	Ca	20	40.08	Plutonium	Pu	94	[242]
Californium	Cf	98	[251*]	Polonium	Po	84	[210*]
Carbon	C	6	12.01115	Potassium	K	19	39.102
Cerium	Ce	58	140.12	Praseodymium	Pr	59	140.907
Cesium	Cs	55	132.905	Promethium	Pm	61	[147*]
Chlorine	Cl	17	35.453	Protactinium	Pa	91	[231]
Chromium	Cr	24	51.996	Radium	Ra	88	[226]
Cobalt	Co	27	58.9332	Radon	Rn	86	[222]
Copper	Cu	29	63.54	Rhenium	Re	75	186.2
Curium	Cm	96	[247]	Rhodium	Rh	45	102.905
Dysprosium	Dy	66	162.50	Rubidium	Rb	37	85.47
Einsteinium	Es	99	[254]	Ruthenium	Ru	44	101.07
Erbium	Er	68	167.26	Samarium	Sm	62	150.35
Europium	Eu	63	151.96	Scandium	Sc	21	44.956
Fermium	Fm	100	[253]	Selenium	Se	34	78.96
Fluorine	F	9	18.9984	Silicon	Si	14	28.086
Francium	Fr	87	[223]	Silver	Ag	47	107.870
Gadolinium	Gd	64	157.25	Sodium	Na	11	22.9898
Gallium	Ga	31	69.72	Strontium	Sr	38	87.62
Germanium	Ge	32	72.59	Sulfur	S	16	32.064
Gold	Au	79	196.967	Tantalum	Ta	73	180.948
Hafnium	Hf	72	178.49	Technetium	Tc	43	[99*]
Helium	He	2	4.0026	Tellurium	Te	52	127.60
Holimum	Ho	67	164.930	Terbium	Tb	65	158.924
Hydrogen	H	1	1.00797	Thallium	Tl	81	204.37
Indium	In	49	114.82	Thorium	Th	90	232.038
Iodine	I	53	126.9044	Thulium	Tm	69	168.934
Iridium	Ir	77	192.2	Tin	Sn	50	118.69
Iron	Fe	26	55.847	Titanium	Ti	22	47.90
Krypton	Kr	36	83.80	Tungsten	W	74	183.85
Lanthanum	La	57	138.91	Uranium	U	92	238.03
Lawrencium	Lw	103	[257]	Vanadium	V	23	50.942
Lead	Pb	82	207.19	Xenon	Xe	54	131.30
Lithium	Li	3	6.939	Ytterbium	Yb	70	173.04
Lutetium	Lu	71	174.97	Yttrium	Y	39	88.905
Magnesium	Mg	12	24.312	Zinc	Zn	30	65.37
Manganese	Mn	25	54.9380	Zirconium	Zr	40	91.22
Mendelevium	Md	101	[256]				

It obviously wasn't enough to list the numbers of atoms in a molecule. Those atoms must be arranged in some particular way. Therefore, even if you had the same number of the same kinds of atoms in two different molecules, they might be *arranged* in different ways. That was what made the molecules different.

But how could the chemists work out the ways in which atoms were arranged in molecules, when both atoms and molecules were too small to see?

The first step forward was taken by an English chemist, Edward Frankland. He combined organic molecules with certain metals, and he found that the atom of a particular metal always combined with a particular number of organic molecules.

In 1852, he suggested that each different kind of atom must have the power of combining with no more than a certain number of other atoms. Each kind of atom had a certain "valence" (VAY-lens), from a Latin word meaning "power."

For instance, hydrogen has a valence of one. A hydrogen atom can combine with only one other atom. Oxygen has a valence of two, so it can combine with two other atoms. Nitrogen has a valence of three; carbon has a valence of four; and so on.

In 1858, a Scottish chemist, Archibald Scott Couper, suggested that each atom be looked on as though it had a number of "bonds" by which it could attach itself to other atoms. Since hydrogen had a valence of one, the hydrogen atom had one bond, which could be written as H—. In the same way, oxygen with a valence of two, nitrogen with three, and carbon with four could be written as

$$-O-, \quad -N-, \quad \text{and} \quad -\overset{\displaystyle |}{\underset{\displaystyle |}{C}}-.$$

You could then build up molecules by attaching the bonds between atoms, getting something that looks almost like a Tinkertoy. Thus, a hydrogen molecule, made up of two hydrogen atoms, would be H—H, each atom holding on to the other by its one bond. Sometimes more than one bond could be used to connect two atoms. The oxygen molecule and the nitrogen molecule are $O{=}O$ and $N{\equiv}N$.

When different atoms are involved, you have the H_2O of water written as H—O—H, the NH_3 of ammonia as H—N—H, the CO_2 of carbon dixoide as
$$\overset{\displaystyle |}{H}$$

$O{=}C{=}O$, and so on.

Sometimes some of the bonds are not used. Carbon monoxide is CO, which can be written $C{=}O$. The oxygen atom has only two bonds and they are used up, but the carbon atom has four bonds, and two of them are not being used. However, carbon monoxide burns easily, combining with oxygen, picking up an oxygen atom for each pair of unused bonds and becoming carbon dioxide.

The method of using atom bonds to build up molecules was easily applied to the small inorganic compounds. It was, however, the large and confusing organic molecules that needed to be worked with.

Kekulé struggled to apply the valence theory to organic compounds, and in 1858 he presented his results. He showed that, by concentrating on the fact that carbon atoms had four bonds each, he could make sense out of a number of molecules whose structures had until then been puzzling.

In order to make sure he was on the right track, he had to be certain of the atomic weights of each element he used. That was one reason he arranged the First International Chemical Congress. Once Cannizzaro got the matter of atomic weights straightened out, Kekulé was sure he was on the right track.

For instance, the molecule of acetic (uh-SEE-tik) acid, which gives vinegar its sour taste, is $C_2H_4O_2$. By the Kekulé system its formula is:

$$\begin{array}{ccc} H & O & \\ | & \| & \\ H-C-C-O-H \\ | & & \\ H & & \end{array}$$

Notice that each carbon atom has four bonds attached to it, each oxygen atom has two, and each hydrogen atom has one.

Octane (OK-tayn), one of the compounds in gasoline, is C_8H_{18} and isopropyl (EYE-soh-PROH-pil) alcohol, or "rubbing alcohol," is C_3H_8O. By the Kekulé system, their formulas are:

$$\begin{array}{cccccccc} H & H & H & H & H & H & H & H \\ | & | & | & | & | & | & | & | \\ H-C-C-C-C-C-C-C-C-H \\ | & | & | & | & | & | & | & | \\ H & H & H & H & H & H & H & H \end{array}$$

Octane

$$
\begin{array}{ccccc}
\text{H} & & \text{H} & & \text{H} \\
| & & | & & | \\
\text{H} & - \text{C} - & \text{C} & - \text{C} - & \text{H} \\
| & & | & & | \\
\text{H} & & \text{O} & & \text{H} \\
& & | \\
& & \text{H}
\end{array}
$$

Isopropyl alcohol

Using Kekulé's system, you can even begin to explain isomers. For instance, ethyl alcohol (the alcohol that is found in wine) has the formula C_2H_6O. Another organic compound, dimethyl ether, which is altogether different from ethyl alcohol, also has the formula C_2H_6O.

By Kekulé's system, there are exactly two different ways in which you can arrange two carbon atoms, six hydrogen atoms, and one oxygen atom:

$$
\begin{array}{ccc}
\text{H} & & \text{H} \\
| & & | \\
\text{H} - \text{C} - \text{O} - \text{C} - \text{H} \\
| & & | \\
\text{H} & & \text{H}
\end{array}
\quad \text{or} \quad
\begin{array}{ccc}
\text{H} & & \text{H} \\
| & & | \\
\text{H} - \text{C} - \text{C} - \text{O} - \text{H} \\
| & & | \\
\text{H} & & \text{H}
\end{array}
$$

In both cases, you have two carbon atoms, each with four bonds; one oxygen atom, with two bonds; and six hydrogen atoms, each with one bond. One of these formulas must stand for ethyl alcohol and the other for dimethyl ether, but which is which?

In one case, you will notice that all the hydrogen atoms are attached to carbon atoms, so all those hydrogen atoms should act in the same way. In the other case, one of the hydrogen atoms is attached to an oxygen atom, so that one hydrogen atom should act differently from the others. It was found that, in ethyl alcohol, one of the hydrogen atoms acts differently from the rest. Therefore, ethyl alcohol must have the formula

$$
\begin{array}{ccc}
& H & H \\
& | & | \\
H- & C- & C-O-H \\
& | & | \\
& H & H
\end{array}
$$

and dimethyl ether must have the other formula.

Many problems involving organic compounds began to be solved quickly once Kekulé announced his system. One simple compound remained a puzzle, however. That was benzene (BEN-zeen), which has the formula C_6H_6. There seemed to be no way of combining six carbon atoms and six hydrogen atoms by the Kekulé system to make a molecule that would be expected to behave as benzene did.

Kekulé puzzled over the problem but got nowhere. Then, one day in 1865, he was riding on a horse-drawn bus and fell into a doze. While half-asleep, he seemed to see a chain of carbon atoms whizzing past him. Suddenly, the tail end of one chain attached itself to the head end to form a ring of atoms. Kekulé snapped awake and knew he had the answer.

48

The formula for benzene looks like this:

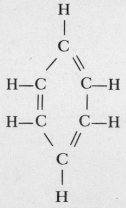

In 1874, a Dutch chemist, Jacobus Henricus Van't Hoff, showed how the bonds of the carbon atom might be placed in actual space, not just drawn on a piece of paper. It became possible to make three-dimensional models of molecules, with all the atoms in the right place and all the bonds pointing in the right direction.

MODEL OF BENZENE

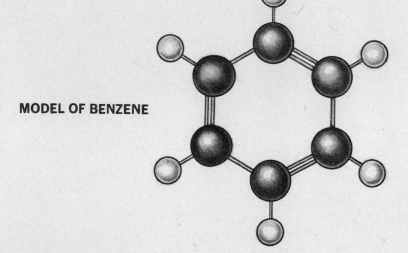

5 The Reality of Atoms

BY THE END of the 1800s, the atomic theory had won all its battles. More and more molecules were being worked out in detail, even some pretty complicated organic ones.

Chemists used Kekulé's system to guide them in putting together atoms to form new molecules that didn't exist in nature. Such "synthetic (sin-THET-ik) molecules" could sometimes be used as dyes or as perfumes or as medicines.

But still no one had ever seen an atom or a molecule. Atoms and molecules remained just ways of explaining what chemists found. They were very handy notions, but no one knew what atoms or molecules were really like, how big they were, how much they weighed, how they were shaped, or anything else. A Russian-German chemist, Friedrich Wilhelm Ostwald (OHST-vald), who was a good friend of Van't Hoff, said that atoms shouldn't be taken too seriously. They were a useful idea, but nothing else. Even though his friend, Van't Hoff, had worked out

51

ways of preparing models of molecules, Ostwald insisted that there was no evidence that atoms *really* existed.

Was there any way of persuading Ostwald that atoms existed?

Back in 1827, a Scottish botanist named Robert Brown was using a microscope to look at tiny particles of pollen floating in water. He noticed that the little pieces of pollen moved about this way and that in every direction. Of course, pollen grains come from plants and have little specks of life in them, so Brown thought the pieces might be moving because they were alive.

Brown tried the same experiment, however, with tiny dye particles, which were definitely not living. They moved in exactly the same way. Such motion this way and that is called "Brownian motion." For over thirty years, no one knew how to explain it.

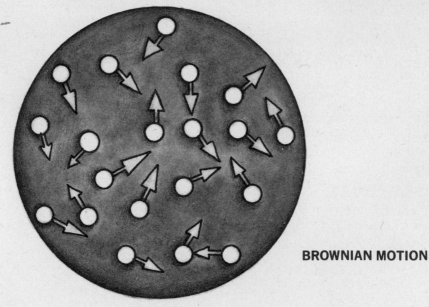

BROWNIAN MOTION

About 1860, a Scottish mathematician, James Clerk Maxwell, studied the behavior of gases. He showed that not only must they be made up of atoms or molecules, but these atoms or molecules must be moving in all directions all the time, and they must be bouncing off each other. The higher the temperature, the faster the atoms or molecules moved and the harder they bounced.

In liquids like water, the molecules are always moving and bouncing, too, though not as easily as in gases.

Anything which is surrounded by water is constantly being struck by atoms or molecules from all sides. There are just about the same number of collisions from opposite sides, so that the collisions mostly balance each other. There may be a few more from one direction than another, but atoms and molecules are so light that a few more collisions this way or that make no difference if the object being struck is fairly large.

But suppose you have a very tiny particle in water. It is being struck from all directions and, when a few more water molecules hit from one direction or another, the tiny particle gets a sizable blow. First there may be a few extra collisions from one direction, then from another, then from still another, and so on. The particle is shoved first in one direction, then in another, then in still another, and so on.

The tiny particle jiggles this way and that endlessly, according to the direction from which the molecular collisions happen to come. That is the explanation of Brownian motion.

In 1905, a German-born mathematician, Albert Einstein, took up the problem of particles moving by Brownian motion. It seemed to him that the smaller the moving particle is, the more easily it would be pushed around by the colliding molecules and the farther it would be pushed away from its original position in a certain amount of time. Again, the larger the moving molecules, the more easily they would push the particle and the farther they would push it.

Einstein worked out a complicated mathematical expression that involved the size of the particle, the size of the water molecule, the distance the particle moved in a certain length of time, and so on. If someone could determine the figures for all the different parts of the mathematical expression, except for the size of the water molecule, that size could then be calculated.

In 1908, a French scientist, Jean Baptiste Perrin (peh-RAN), tackled the problem. He put small particles of something called gum resin in a container of water. Gravity pulled the particles to the bottom of the container, but Brownian motion kept pushing them upward.

According to Einstein's mathematical expression, the number of particles in the water ought to get less and less by a certain amount as one went up from the bottom. Perrin counted the particles at various heights and was able to supply numbers for everything in Einstein's mathematical expression except the size of the water molecule. Then he could calculate its size.

ALBERT EINSTEIN—ABOUT 1905

For the first time, the size of the water molecule and of the atoms that made it up was worked out. It turned out that an atom is about 1/250,000,000th of an inch across. That means that if two hundred fifty million atoms were placed side by side, they would form a line one inch long.

It also meant that in a pint of water there are about fifteen trillion trillion water molecules. Fifteen trillion trillion can be written like this: 15,000,000,000,000,000,000,000,000. If a single drop of water was divided equally among all the four billion people in the whole world, each person would get nearly four trillion (4,000,000,000,000) molecules.

Ostwald had to give in when the news of Perrin's experiment arrived. Brownian motion certainly made it possible for a person to see individual molecules at work. Even though the molecules themselves couldn't be seen, the results of their jiggling, pushing, and colliding could be seen. Thus, thanks to Perrin, there came a clear proof as to how large individual atoms were.

After that, virtually every scientist was sure that atoms really existed and that they weren't just a handy notion.

In 1936, a German scientist named Erwin Wilhelm Mueller invented a "field-emission microscope." This made use of a very fine needle-tip in a container from which all the air had been removed (a "vacuum").

When heated, the needle-tip gave off tiny particles, which moved away from the tip in straight lines and hit a screen covered with chemicals that glowed

FIELD-EMISSION MICROSCOPE

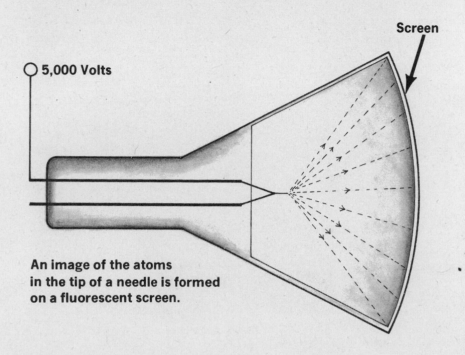

Screen

5,000 Volts

**An image of the atoms
in the tip of a needle is formed
on a fluorescent screen.**

when the particles struck them. From the glow, a person could tell what kind of structure the needle-tip had.

Mueller improved this device and by the 1950s he could take photographs of the glowing screen, which showed the individual atoms making up the needle-tip, all neatly lined up.

Atoms in a crystal of tungsten appear as small luminous dots on the screen of a field-emission microscope.

Finally, people actually *saw* atoms. By the time they did, though, they knew that atoms were not what they had once been thought to be. Leucippus and Democritus had thought that atoms were unbreakable objects and the smallest things possible. (Remember that the very word "atom" means "unbreakable.")

Dalton had thought the same thing and, all through the 1800s, chemists had been sure that the atoms were the smallest things there were. They imagined atoms to be tiny little balls, hard and smooth, which couldn't be marked or broken.

Then, as the 1800s ended, it was found that this was not so after all. The atom was made up of many kinds of still smaller "sub-atomic particles." One important sub-atomic particle is the "electron." It is only 1/1837th as heavy as the hydrogen atom, which is the smallest atom. The particles given off by the fine needle-tip of Mueller's first field-emission microscope were electrons.

Nowadays scientists know that atoms contain a tiny nucleus at their very center. This tiny nucleus weighs almost as much as the entire atom. Around it are a number of very light electrons. The way in which scientists discovered what the inside of atoms looked like is a complicated story. It will have to be told in another book.

Index